D1273766

INSIDE THE NHL

New York
RANGERS

Claryssa
Lozano

AV² provides enriched content that supplements and complements this book. Weigl's AV² books strive to create inspired learning and engage young minds in a total learning experience.

Your AV² Media Enhanced books come alive with...

Audio
Listen to sections of the book read aloud.

Key Words
Study vocabulary, and complete a matching word activity.

Go to **www.av2books.com**, and enter this book's unique code.

Video
Watch informative video clips.

Quizzes
Test your knowledge.

BOOK CODE

H768564

Embedded Weblinks
Gain additional information for research.

Slide Show
View images and captions, and prepare a presentation.

AV² by Weigl brings you media enhanced books that support active learning.

Try This!
Complete activities and hands-on experiments.

... and much, much more!

Published by AV² by Weigl
350 5th Avenue, 59th Floor
New York, NY 10118
Websites: www.av2books.com   www.weigl.com

Library of Congress Control Number: 2014951950

ISBN 978-1-4896-3164-0 (hardcover)
ISBN 978-1-4896-3165-7 (single-user eBook)
ISBN 978-1-4896-3166-4 (multi-user eBook)

Printed in the United States of America in Brainerd, Minnesota
1 2 3 4 5 6 7 8 9 0   19 18 17 16 15

032015
WEP050315

Senior Editor Heather Kissock
Art Director Terry Paulhus

Photo Credits
Every reasonable effort has been made to trace ownership and to obtain permission to reprint copyright material. The publishers would be pleased to have any errors or omissions brought to their attention so that they may be corrected in subsequent printings.

Weigl acknowledges Getty Images and iStock as its primary image suppliers for this title.

New York
RANGERS

CONTENTS

Introduction

The New York Rangers joined the National Hockey League (NHL) in 1926 as one of the **Original Six**. However, it was the New York Americans that first brought hockey to the New York area one year earlier. The Rangers had to be at least as competitive and entertaining as the Americans in order to earn a place in New Yorkers' hearts. The Rangers were winners right away, and then some. They shocked hockey fans everywhere when they won the Stanley Cup in just their second season.

Before he became coach, Frank Boucher played for the Rangers for 13 seasons.

After winning the Cup in 1928, the Rangers did not slow down. They made the **playoffs** in nine straight seasons and won another Cup five years later in 1933. The Rangers have reached the finals 11 times and have won the Stanley Cup four times. Although they have not won the Cup since 1994, the Rangers made it back to the Stanley Cup Final in the 2013–2014 season, where they fell short, losing in five games to the Los Angeles Kings.

Chris Kreider was one of two Rangers to score a goal during the last game of the 2013–2014 finals.

New York RANGERS

Arena Madison Square Garden

Division Metropolitan

Head Coach Alain Vigneault

Location New York, New York

NHL Stanley Cup Titles 1928, 1933, 1940, 1994

Nicknames Blueshirts, Tex's Rangers

56
Playoff appearances

2
Conference Championships

8
Retired Numbers

4
Hart Trophies

History

40

former Rangers are in the Hockey Hall of Fame.

Bun Cook was a key member of the 1928 and 1933 Rangers Stanley Cup championship teams. The speedy left wing was part of the "Bread Line," skating alongside his brother Bill, and Frank Boucher.

In 1926, Madison Square Garden President Tex Rickard brought another hockey team, the Rangers, to New York City when he was awarded a **franchise** by the NHL. He had seen how popular the New York Americans had become and wanted to start a team of his own. Knowing the team had to be extremely talented in order to gain its own fans, Rickard hired university hockey coach Conn Smythe to build the new hockey team. Smythe brought in strong players such as Bill Cook, Frank Boucher, Ching Johnson, and Taffy Abel.

The Rangers were nearly unstoppable during their first nine seasons in the NHL, qualifying for the playoffs every single season and winning two Stanley Cups. Over the years, some of the greatest players to lace up a pair of skates played on the ice at Madison Square Garden. In total, the Rangers have had 60 Hall of Fame players and coaches during a history that spans close to a century. During that time, perhaps the greatest season was 1993–1994. The team scored 112 points that year, the most in Rangers history, and captured the Cup for the first time in 54 seasons.

Conn Smythe has a trophy named in his honor that is awarded to the most valuable player during the postseason.

The Arena

The current Rangers arena is the fourth Madison Square Garden to have been built.

In 1964, the construction of the world famous Madison Square Garden on 33rd Street in New York City was officially underway. The original arena, home to the Rangers for 40 seasons, and also known as Madison Square Garden, had been on 50th Street. The arena was relocated so that it would be surrounded by other iconic sites, such as the Empire State Building, Central Park, and Rockefeller Center. Four years after construction began, the Rangers made the arena their home. In February, 1968, the Rangers skated onto the ice for their first game at the new Madison Square Garden.

Dedicated Rangers fans followed their team to their new arena and sellouts became routine. Since the team's opening season, Rangers games have averaged more than 15,000 fans per contest. With the exception of the 2012–2013 season, the Rangers have had an average game day attendance of more than 18,000 fans for nearly two decades. Madison Square Garden is currently the oldest NHL arena. In recent years, it was ranked fifth on a list of most expensive arenas in the world, at $1.1 billion.

Rangers fans line up for a "stacked high" pastrami, corned beef, and turkey sandwich at the Carnegie Deli, located inside Madison Square Garden.

Where They Play

British Columbia

Alberta

CANADA

Saskatchewan

Manitoba

Ontario

Washington

Montana

North Dakota

Minnesota

Wisconsin

Oregon

Idaho

South Dakota

Wyoming

Iowa

Illinois

UNITED

Nevada

Utah

Colorado

Nebraska

STATES

Kansas

Missouri

California

Oklahoma

Arkansas

Arizona

New Mexico

Pacific Ocean

MEXICO

Texas

Louisiana

Missi...

Gulf of Mexico

NHL WESTERN CONFERENCE

PACIFIC DIVISION

1 Anaheim Ducks
2 Arizona Coyotes
3 Calgary Flames
4 Edmonton Oilers
5 Los Angeles Kings
6 San Jose Sharks
7 Vancouver Canucks

CENTRAL DIVISION

8 Chicago Blackhawks
9 Colorado Avalanche
10 Dallas Stars
11 Minnesota Wild
12 Nashville Predators
13 St. Louis Blues
14 Winnipeg Jets

MADISON SQUARE GARDEN
THE WORLD'S MOST FAMOUS ARENA®

Arena
Madison Square Garden

Location
Four Pennsylvania Plaza
New York, NY 10001

Broke Ground
October 29, 1964

Completed
February 11, 1968

Features
- Two "Chase Bridges" that run above the ice
- Two 600-square foot (55.7-square meter) video screens on the ceiling
- State-of-the-art scoreboard
- Six 145-inch screens on each bridge
- 18,200 seats

LEGEND
☆ Madison Square Garden
■ Eastern Conference
■ Western Conference

NHL EASTERN CONFERENCE

ATLANTIC DIVISION
15 Boston Bruins
16 Buffalo Sabres
17 Detroit Red Wings
18 Florida Panthers
19 Montreal Canadiens
20 Ottawa Senators
21 Tampa Bay Lightning
22 Toronto Maple Leafs

METROPOLITAN DIVISION
23 Carolina Hurricanes
24 Columbus Blue Jackets
25 New Jersey Devils
26 New York Islanders
☆ 27 New York Rangers
28 Philadelphia Flyers
29 Pittsburgh Penguins
30 Washington Capitals

The Uniforms

8 different player numbers have been retired. The number nine was retired in honor of two Rangers.

The Heritage jersey is mainly navy blue. Along the hemline are the Rangers' numbers that have been retired. The phrase "Established 1926" is printed on the neckline. The right shoulder has a patch that honors the team's 85th anniversary.

HOME

AWAY

Since 1926, the Rangers have remained true to their red, white, and blue color scheme. For their first 25 years in the NHL, their jerseys were always the same, blue with red and white stripes. It was not until 1951 that the team added an alternate white jersey.

In 1996, the team gained another alternate jersey that was dark blue with a new **logo** of the Statue of Liberty on the front. In 2007, the team went back to their classic look of red, white, and blue. The most recent change occurred in 2010 when the Rangers introduced their Heritage Jerseys.

Owner Tex Rickard decided he wanted the Rangers to stand out from the New York Americans, so he made their team name run diagonally across their jerseys. Although the Americans left the NHL in 1942, the Rangers have kept the diagonal pattern on their jerseys to this day.

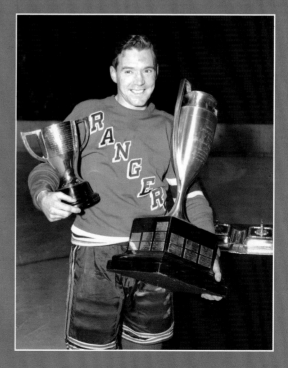

Helmets and Face Masks

RULE 48

bans "blindside hits to a player's head." Though it was meant to assist helmets in protecting players' heads, it did not bring down the number of head injuries.

Goaltender Dave Kerr played in the NHL from 1930–1941, before helmets were required to be worn by goalies.

Wearing a helmet while playing a dangerous sport such as hockey is an important safety measure. Surprisingly, NHL players went decades without wearing them. After countless head injuries and even one death, the NHL finally made it mandatory for new players to wear protective head gear in 1979. In the case of the Rangers, they played 53 seasons before the helmet rule was implemented.

When the team finally did add helmets to its uniform, they were either blue or white to match the Rangers' jerseys. Today, Rangers helmets are bright blue and white with the letters "NYR" in red on each side with each player's number on the back. The blue helmets are worn at home games, while the white ones are worn on the road.

Goalies are allowed a more unique helmet, with more space for creative designs. Current goalie Henrik Lundqvist has the Statue of Liberty on his helmet to honor New York City.

Ed Giacomin was among the first Rangers goalies to wear a face mask. Though it did not have any designs, it worked to protect his face and skull from injury.

The Coaches

2 Lester Patrick's two sons not only played professional hockey, but were also part of the New York Rangers.

Lester Patrick ended his career as a coach with a final record of 281 wins, 216 losses, and 107 ties.

The Rangers have had a total of 40 coaches since 1926, and 14 of them have been inducted into the hockey Hall of Fame. Lester Patrick, Frank Boucher, and Mike Keenan all won Stanley Cups with the Rangers, but it was Patrick and Boucher who impacted the Rangers most during their times as head coach.

LESTER PATRICK Lester Patrick was the first person to coach the Rangers and was their coach for 13 straight seasons. He led the team to Stanley Cup victories in 1928 and 1933. In 1966, the NHL honored him with the Lester Patrick Trophy, which would be presented yearly to someone either active or retired from the game for their outstanding service to the sport of hockey.

FRANK BOUCHER Frank Boucher retired from his professional hockey playing career to become a coach for the Rangers at the start of the 1939–1940 season. In that first season, Boucher led the Rangers to a Stanley Cup championship, beating the Maple Leafs. In 1993, 16 years after his death, Boucher was awarded the Lester Patrick Trophy.

ALAIN VIGNEAULT Current coach Alain Vigneault came to the Rangers after coaching for various teams and leagues the world over. In 2007, he won the Jack Adams Award while coaching the Vancouver Canucks. The award recognized him as the coach who contributed most to his team's success.

Fans and
the Internet

In the 2013–2014 season, the New York Rangers had a home game attendance of 100 percent capacity, with an average attendance of 18,006 fans.

Rangers fans will follow their team wherever they may go. Whether that is to their home ice on 33rd Street, or to any other arena throughout the country, Rangers fans often show up and display their support. However, in the event that they cannot make it to a game, the Rangers website has them covered.

The website directly links fans to a "Blueshirts United" page. On the page, fans can find game stats, videos, articles, player information, tickets, and the season schedule. The Rangers website also has a "Stay Connected" page that directly links fans to the team's Facebook, Instagram, Twitter, and Google+. The site even allows the fans to sign up to receive text message alerts during games.

Signs
of a fan

#1 Rangers fan Larry Goodman arrives at each game ready to pump up the crowd by dancing in section 407.

#2 Like many other sports fans, Rangers fans enjoy painting their face with the team's colors.

Legends of the Past

Many great players have suited up for the Rangers. A few of them have become icons of the team and the city it represents.

Position: Defenseman
NHL Seasons: 18 (1987–2006)
Born: March 3, 1968, in Corpus Christi, Texas, United States

Brian Leetch

Brian Leetch was selected by the New York Rangers during the 1986 NHL **Entry Draft** as the ninth overall pick in the first round. He did not play in his first game with the team until the 1988–1989 season. During that year, Leetch was awarded the Calder Memorial Trophy as the **Rookie** of Year. He went on to win the Conn Smythe Trophy once, and the **Norris Trophy** twice. During the 1993–1994 playoffs, Leetch scored four game-winning goals and helped the team win the Stanley Cup. He was inducted into the Hockey Hall of Fame in 2009.

Mark Messier

Mark Messier began playing in the NHL for the Edmonton Oilers in 1979 but was traded to the Rangers in 1991. At the conclusion of his first season with the Rangers, Messier was awarded both the Hart Memorial Trophy and the Ted Lindsay Award. The awards recognized him as the most valuable and most outstanding player that season. During the 1993–1994 playoffs, Messier scored four game-winning goals and dished out 18 **assists**. He helped the team win its fourth Stanley Cup. Messier became a Hall of Fame member in 2007.

Position: Left Wing, Center
NHL Seasons: 25 (1979–2004)
Born: January 18, 1961, in Edmonton, Alberta, Canada

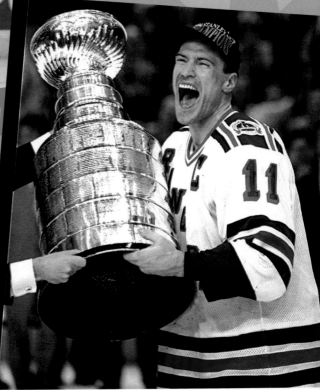

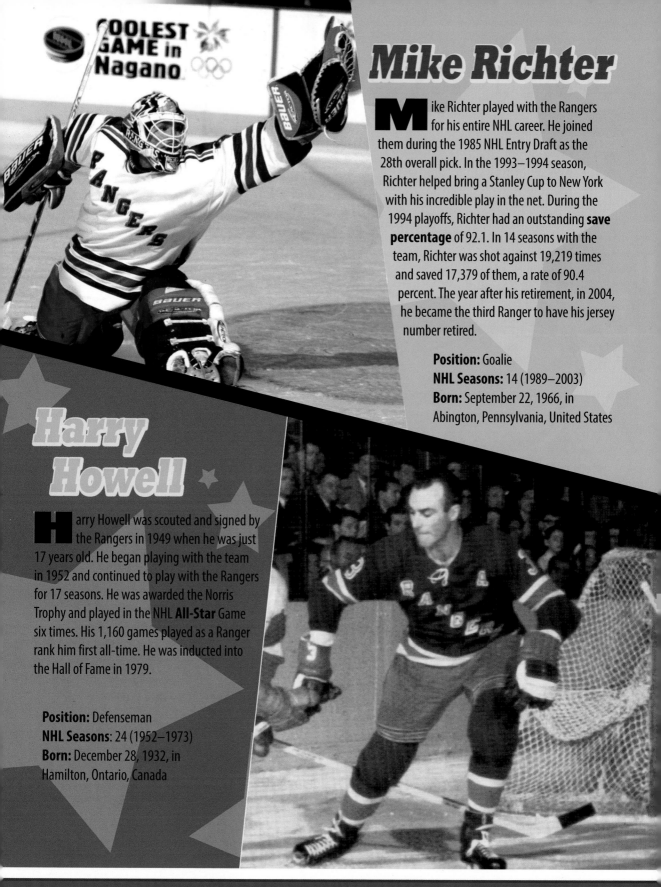

Mike Richter

Mike Richter played with the Rangers for his entire NHL career. He joined them during the 1985 NHL Entry Draft as the 28th overall pick. In the 1993–1994 season, Richter helped bring a Stanley Cup to New York with his incredible play in the net. During the 1994 playoffs, Richter had an outstanding **save percentage** of 92.1. In 14 seasons with the team, Richter was shot against 19,219 times and saved 17,379 of them, a rate of 90.4 percent. The year after his retirement, in 2004, he became the third Ranger to have his jersey number retired.

Position: Goalie
NHL Seasons: 14 (1989–2003)
Born: September 22, 1966, in Abington, Pennsylvania, United States

Harry Howell

Harry Howell was scouted and signed by the Rangers in 1949 when he was just 17 years old. He began playing with the team in 1952 and continued to play with the Rangers for 17 seasons. He was awarded the Norris Trophy and played in the NHL **All-Star** Game six times. His 1,160 games played as a Ranger rank him first all-time. He was inducted into the Hall of Fame in 1979.

Position: Defenseman
NHL Seasons: 24 (1952–1973)
Born: December 28, 1932, in Hamilton, Ontario, Canada

Stars of Today

Today's Rangers team is made up of many young, talented players who have proven that they are among the best in the league.

Henrik Lundqvist

The Rangers drafted Henrik Lundqvist during the seventh round of the 2000 NHL Entry Draft. As a late draft pick, Lundqvist was not expected to shine, and certainly not in his rookie season. In that 2005–2006 rookie season, he recorded a strong save percentage of 92.2 percent. Consistently among the top goalies in the NHL, Lundqvist has been nominated for the Vezina Trophy each of his nine seasons in the league. Lundqvist won the Vezina Trophy as the league's best goaltender in 2012. He has played in three All-Star games and continues to shine as the Rangers' biggest star.

Position: Goalie
NHL Seasons: 9 (2005–2014)
Born: March 2, 1982, in Are, Jamtland, Sweden

Martin St. Louis

After playing with the Tampa Bay Lightning for 13 seasons, Martin St. Louis was dealt to the Rangers during the 2013–2014 season. Traded just in time to compete in the 2014 NHL playoffs, St. Louis made an immediate impact for his new team. He scored a total of eight playoff goals and helped the team reach the Stanley Cup finals. Though they did not win the Cup, St. Louis did his part, proving to be a capable veteran player with a knack for finding the net.

Position: Right Wing
NHL Seasons: 15 (1998–2014)
Born: June 18, 1975, in Laval, Quebec, Canada

Ryan McDonagh

Position: Defenseman
NHL Seasons: 4 (2010–2014)
Born: June 13, 1989, in St. Paul, Minnesota, United States

Though he was drafted by the Montreal Canadiens, Ryan McDonagh played in his first NHL game with the Rangers during 2010–2011 season. During that season, McDonagh played in only 40 games but managed a special moment during his brief stint as he scored a game-winning goal. He reached several career highs with the Rangers during the 2013–2014 season. He scored 14 goals, four of which were game winners, and recorded 29 assists, for a total of 43 points. That same season, McDonagh won the Players' Player Award, and was named team's Most Valuable Player (MVP). McDonagh is the first person since Brian Leetch to have accomplished this feat.

Rick Nash

Rick Nash was the first overall pick by the Columbus Blue Jackets in the 2002 NHL Entry Draft. Nash was then traded to the Rangers during the 2012–2013 season. During his second season in the NHL, Nash was awarded the Maurice Richard Trophy, which goes to the "top goal scorer" in the league. Reliable and productive, Nash has recorded more than 15 goals for 11 straight seasons.

Position: Left Wing
NHL Seasons: 11 (2002–2014)
Born: June 16, 1984, in Brampton, Ontario, Canada

All-Time Records

1,021
Most Points
After 18 seasons in New York, Rod Gilbert is ranked first among all Rangers for most goals scored and overall points. He scored a total of 406 goals and collected 1,021 career points.

51
Most Shutouts
Henrik Lundqvist holds the franchise record for most **shutouts**. Lundqvist's 51 shutouts over nine seasons averages out to 5.55 shutouts per season.

123
Most Single Season Points
The 2005–2006 season saw right winger Jaromir Jagr shatter two franchise records. That season, he collected 123 points while scoring 54 goals.

741
Most Assists

In addition to holding the record for most overall assists as a Ranger, with 741, Brian Leetch holds the record for most assists in a single season, with 80, during the 1991–1992 season.

1,160
Most Games

Over the course of his 17 seasons with the Rangers, Harry Howell played in 1,160 games, more contests than any other player in team history.

Timeline

Throughout the team's history, the Rangers have had many memorable events that have become defining moments for the team and its fans.

1928
Lester Patrick is named coach and general manager of the New York Rangers. He went on to coach the team for 13 seasons.

In 1928, the Rangers win their first Stanley Cup after defeating the Montreal Maroons, 2-1. No other team has ever won the Stanley Cup in its second year as a franchise.

| 1920 | 1925 | 1930 | 1935 | 1940 | 1945 |

1926
Madison Square Garden president, Tex Rickard, is awarded a franchise for the New York Rangers. The team's nickname "Tex's Rangers" is introduced.

1933
The team wins its second Stanley Cup after defeating the Toronto Maple Leafs, 1-0, in overtime. The Rangers made easy work of the series, defeating the Maple Leafs in three of four playoff games.

1940
The New York Rangers win their third Stanley Cup in Toronto. This Stanley Cup is also clinched with an overtime goal.

1968
The Rangers say goodbye to their old home and play in their first game at the new Madison Square Garden.

The Future
After 20 years without a Stanley Cup, the New York Rangers reached the final during the 2013–2014 season and were outlasted in a tight series. The past decade has been a strong one for the Rangers as they have qualified for the playoffs eight times. With a determined coach and a lineup of talented players, the team is ready to not only make it to the finals once more, but to take that final step—as champions.

> In 1994, the team wins its fourth Stanley Cup against the Vancouver Canucks.

| 1965 | 1975 | 1985 | 1995 | 2005 | 2015 |

1966
The Rangers present the Lester Patrick Trophy in honor of the team's first coach, Lester Patrick. The trophy honors a person who has performed outstanding service to the game of hockey.

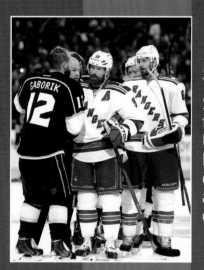

2014
The team reaches the Stanley Cup Final against the Los Angeles Kings. Unfortunately, the Rangers lose Game 5 in double overtime and are eliminated by the champion Kings.

Write a Biography

Life Story

A person's life story can be the subject of a book. This kind of book is called a biography. Biographies often describe the lives of people who have achieved great success. These people may be alive today, or they may have lived many years ago. Reading a biography can help you learn more about a great person.

Get the Facts

Use this book, and research in the library and on the internet, to find out more about your favorite Ranger. Learn as much about this player as you can. What position does he play? What are his statistics in important categories? Has he set any records? Also, be sure to write down key events in the person's life. What was his childhood like? What has he accomplished off the field? Is there anything else that makes this person special or unusual?

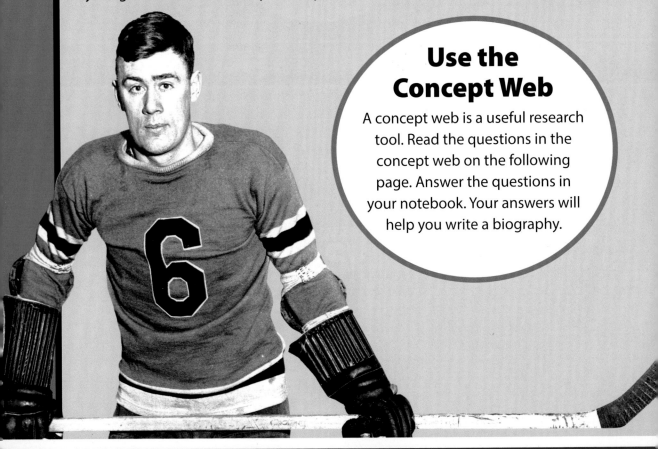

Use the Concept Web

A concept web is a useful research tool. Read the questions in the concept web on the following page. Answer the questions in your notebook. Your answers will help you write a biography.

Concept Web

Adulthood
- Where does this individual currently reside?
- Does he or she have a family?

Your Opinion
- What did you learn from the books you read in your research?
- Would you suggest these books to others?
- Was anything missing from these books?

Childhood
- Where and when was this person born?
- Describe his or her parents, siblings, and friends.
- Did this person grow up in unusual circumstances?

Accomplishments off the Field
- What is this person's life's work?
- Has he or she received awards or recognition for accomplishments?
- How have this person's accomplishments served others?

Write a Biography

Help and Obstacles
- Did this individual have a positive attitude?
- Did he or she receive help from others?
- Did this person have a mentor?
- Did this person face any hardships?
- If so, how were the hardships overcome?

Accomplishments on the Field
- What records does this person hold?
- What key games and plays have defined his career?
- What are his stats in categories important to his position?

Work and Preparation
- What was this person's education?
- What was his or her work experience?
- How does this person work?
- What is the process he or she uses?

Trivia Time

Take this quiz to test your knowledge of the Rangers. The answers are printed upside down under each question.

1 What are the Rangers' team colors?

A. red, blue, and white

2 How many players have had their number retired?

A. Eight

3 How many Madison Square Garden arenas have been built?

A. Four

4 Which coach led the Rangers to the most Stanley Cups?

A. Lester Patrick

5 How many times have the Rangers made it to the playoffs?

A. 56

6 How many Rangers' coaches have reached the Hall of Fame?

A. 14

7 When were helmets made mandatory for new NHL players?

A. 1979

8 Which player holds the record for most goals ever scored as a Ranger?

A. Rod Gilbert

9 Who is the current coach of the Rangers?

A. Alain Vigneault

Key Words

All-Star: a game made for the best-ranked players in the NHL that happens mid-season. A player can be named an All-Star and then be sent to play in this game.

assists: a statistic that is attributed to up to two players of the scoring team who shoot, pass, or deflect the puck toward the scoring teammate

entry draft: an annual meeting where different teams in the NHL are allowed to pick new, young players who can join their teams

franchise: a team that is a member of a professional sports league

logo: a symbol that stands for a team or organization

Norris Trophy: short for the James Norris Memorial Trophy, this trophy is awarded to the "defenseman who demonstrates throughout the season the greatest all-round ability in the position"

Original Six: the first six hockey teams that made up the NHL before the league expanded in 1967

playoffs: a series of games that occur after regular season play

rookie: a player age 26 or younger who has played no more than 25 games in a previous season, nor six or more games in two previous seasons

save percentage: the rate at which a goalie stops shots being made toward his net by the opposing team

shutouts: games in which the losing team is blocked from making any goals

Index

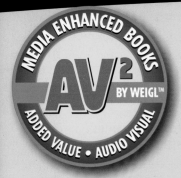

Log on to www.av2books.com

AV² by Weigl brings you media enhanced books that support active learning. Go to www.av2books.com, and enter the special code found on page 2 of this book. You will gain access to enriched and enhanced content that supplements and complements this book. Content includes video, audio, weblinks, quizzes, a slide show, and activities.

AV² Online Navigation

Audio
Listen to sections of the book read aloud.

Book Pages
AV² pages directly correspond to pages in the book.

Video
Watch informative video clips.

Key Words
Study vocabulary, and complete a matching word activity.

Embedded Weblinks
Gain additional information for research.

Quizzes
Test your knowledge.

Slide Show
View images and captions, and prepare a presentation.

Try This!
Complete activities and hands-on experiments.

AV² was built to bridge the gap between print and digital. We encourage you to tell us what you like and what you want to see in the future.

Sign up to be an AV² Ambassador at www.av2books.com/ambassador.